# Read and Play
# Pets

by Jim Pipe

Stargazer Books

**pet**

Here is a **pet**.

3

cat

A **cat** is a pet.

5

**dog**

A **dog** is a pet, too.

7

**rabbit**

8

A **rabbit** is a furry pet.

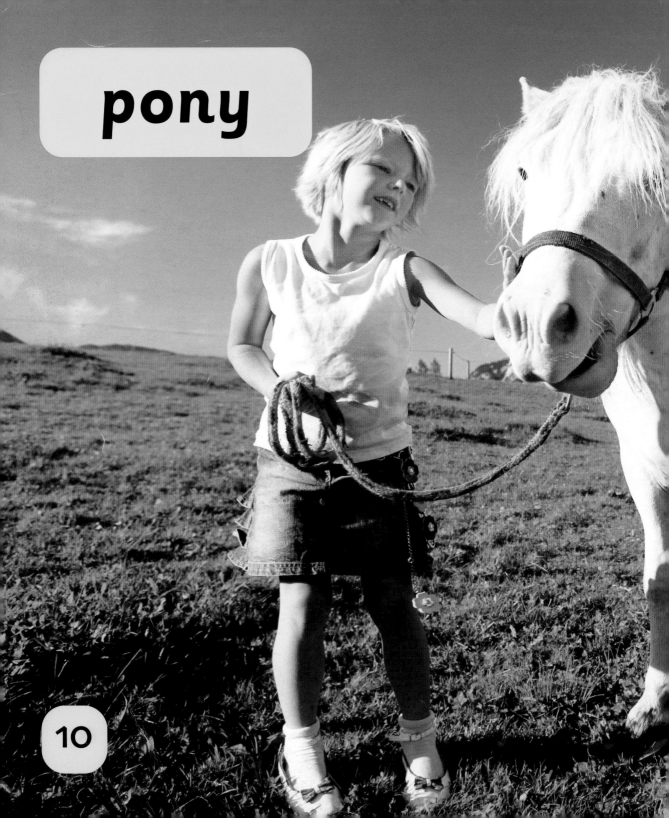

pony

A **pony** is a big pet.

11

**hamster**

A **hamster** is a small pet.

13

# guinea pig

A **guinea pig** is a small pet, too.

14

tortoise

16

A **tortoise** is a pet.

17

goldfish

A **goldfish** is a pet.
It swims.

19

# Who am I?

pony

rabbit

cat

goldfish

20

Match the words and pictures.

# How many?

Can you count the yellow fish?

21

# Odd pets

**Snake**

**Spider**

**Monkey**

**Lizard**

Would you like these as pets?

# Index

# For Parents and Teachers

## Questions you could ask:

*p. 2 What is this pet?* It is a rabbit. Rabbits need space (such as a backyard or run) to hop around and stand up on their hind legs.

*p. 4 What is this cat doing?* It is resting. Pets that are busy at night, such as cats, mice, and hamsters, often sleep during the day.

*p. 6 Do you like dogs?* Dogs make very good pets – they can be friendly, clever, playful, and cuddly!

*p. 8 What is this rabbit doing?* It is nibbling the grass. The best food for rabbits is grass or hay and they also need plenty of fresh water. Also, point out its white tail and long ears.

*p. 10 Would you like to ride a pony?* Riding is fun but looking after a pony is hard work! They need to be fed and groomed and their stables kept clean.

*p. 12 What does a hamster feel like?* Soft and furry. Compare with other pets, e.g. tortoise.

*p. 16 What does a tortoise have on its back?* A shell. This protects its soft body underneath.

*p. 18 Where does a pet fish live?* A fish lives in water, e.g. in a pond or aquarium.

## Activities you could do:

• Role play: ask the reader to act out how they would look after their favorite pet, e.g. feeding, grooming, washing, playing with them.

• Introduce pets by singing "How Much Is That Doggy/Kitty in the Window" and other songs.

• Play a game of "Simon says" where the trainer gives a pet commands such as sit, stand, jump, roll over, lie down, etc.

• Encourage the reader to make a model home for a pet made out of cardboard or straws. Cotton can be used for bedding inside.

• Use medical play items and stuffed animal pets to set up an imaginary vet clinic for pets.

• Create three zones on table, e.g. farm, zoo, and pet zones. Cut out pictures of different animals and ask readers to put each animal in the correct zone(s).

© Aladdin Books Ltd 2008

**Designed and produced by**
Aladdin Books Ltd

All rights reserved

Printed in the United States

**Series consultant**
Zoe Stillwell is an experienced preschool teacher.

**First published in 2008**
in the United States
by Stargazer Books
c/o The Creative Company
123 South Broad Street
P.O. Box 227
Mankato, Minnesota 56002

**Photocredits:**
l-left, r-right, b-bottom, t-top,
c-center, m-middle
All photos on cover and insides
from istockphoto.com except: 2-3,
23tl & bl—Comstock. 22tl—
Photodisc. 22bl , 23mlb—John Foxx.
23mlt, mrt, mrb & rb—Ingram.

Library of Congress Cataloging-in-Publication Data

Pipe, Jim, 1966-
  Pets / by Jim Pipe.
      p. cm. -- (Read and play)
  Includes bibliographical references and Index.
  ISBN 978-1-59604-162-2 (alk. paper)
      1. Pets--Juvenile literature.
I. Title.

SF416.2.P57 2007
636.088'7--dc22

2007007755